Mice

Nocturnal Explorers

Rebecca Rissman

raintree

a Capstone company — publishers for children

Raintree is an imprint of Capstone Global Library
Limited, a company incorporated in England and Wales
having its registered office at 7 Pilgrim Street, London,
EC4V 6LB – Registered company number: 6695582

www.raintreepublishers.co.uk
myorders@raintreepublishers.co.uk

Text © Capstone Global Library Limited 2015
First published in hardback in 2014
First published in paperback in 2015
The moral rights of the proprietor have been asserted.

Edited by Brynn Baker, Clare Lewis,
       and Helen Cox Cannons
Designed by Kyle Grenz and Tim Bond
Picture research by Tracy Cummins
Production by Helen McCreath
Originated by Capstone Global Library Limited
Printed and bound in China by Leo Paper Group

ISBN 978-1-406-28282-5 (hardback)
18 17 16 15 14
10 9 8 7 6 5 4 3 2 1

ISBN 978-1-406-28289-4 (paperback)
19 18 17 16 15
10 9 8 7 6 5 4 3 2 1

British Library Cataloguing in Publication Data
A full catalogue record for this book is available from
the British Library.

Acknowledgements
We would like to thank the following for permission
to reproduce photographs: Alamy: © Arterra Picture
Library, 6, 23d, © Chris Lishman, 15, © David Chapman,
10, 18, © Evgeny Drobzhev, 21, © Redmond Durrell, 17,
© tbkmedia.de, 22, © TOPICMedia/ L. Lenz, 13, 23e;
Ardea: © Werner Curth, 11; FLPA: Derek Middleton, 5,
back cover, Gerard Lacz, 16, Hugo Willcox/FN/Minden,
4, Imagebroker, 7 owl, J.-L. Klein & M.-/Biosphoto, 14,
23b, Michael Durham/Minden Pictures, 7 bat; Getty
Images: Ivan Bajic, 20; naturepl.com: © Elliott Bignell,
19, 23c, © Philippe Clement, 9, 23a; Shutterstock:
Andrew Astbury, 7 fox, Piotr Krzeslak, 7 hedgehog;
Superstock: Flirt, front cover, Biosphoto, 12.

Every effort has been made to contact copyright holders
of material reproduced in this book. Any omissions will
be rectified in subsequent printings if notice is given to
the publisher.

All the Internet addresses (URLs) given in this book
were valid at the time of going to press. However, due to
the dynamic nature of the Internet, some addresses may
have changed, or sites may have changed or ceased to
exist since publication. While the author and publisher
regret any inconvenience this may cause readers, no
responsibility for any such changes can be accepted by
either the author or the publisher.

Contents

What is a mouse?. 4

What does nocturnal mean? 6

Where do mice live? 8

What do mice eat? 10

Do mice have predators? 12

What are baby mice like? 14

What do mice do in winter? 16

How can you spot mice?. 18

How can you help mice?. 20

Mouse body map 22

Picture glossary 23

Find out more. 24

Index 24

What is a mouse?

A mouse is a small **mammal** that has a long tail and large ears.

It has short legs with sharp claws.

You might wonder why you rarely see mice during the day.

This is because they are **nocturnal**.

What does nocturnal mean?

Nocturnal animals are awake at night.

Animals that are nocturnal sleep during the day.

Many different animals are nocturnal.

Bats, owls, hedgehogs, and foxes are nocturnal.

Where do mice live?

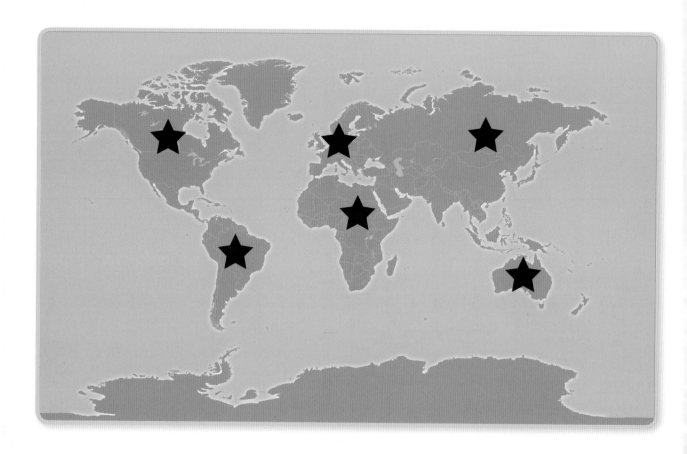

Mice live in almost every country in the world.

They live in forests, fields, gardens, and even in some homes.

Mice dig **burrows** to stay safe and dry.

They make nests inside their burrows with sticks and leaves.

What do mice eat?

Mice eat seeds, berries, nuts, and roots.

They sometimes eat insects too.

Mice living near humans may eat fruits and vegetables in gardens.

They may also eat from rubbish bins.

Do mice have predators?

Mice have many **predators**.

Weasels, owls, and foxes hunt mice for food.

Cats hunt mice for food.

Humans trap and kill mice too.

What are baby mice like?

One to four times a year, female mice give birth to a **litter** of babies.

Mice litters usually have between two and seven babies.

Baby mice are blind and almost hairless.

After about a month, they are big enough to go out on their own.

What do mice do in winter?

Mice spend time in their nests during winter.

Sometimes, many mice share the same nest.

In very cold weather, some mice will move into buildings.

They make nests in quiet corners of homes, barns, and garages.

How can you spot mice?

Mice are most active at night.

Look for small, black mouse droppings.
They can tell you where mice have been.

In the dark, listen for soft rustling.

It could be the sound of mice!

How can you help mice?

Do not feed mice. They find plenty of food on their own.

Keep your rubbish bins covered. Rubbish sometimes makes mice sick.

Do not touch wild mice. They bite!

Mice can carry diseases that make people sick. If you see a mouse, tell an adult.

Mouse body map

eye

body

nose

tail

whisker

Picture glossary

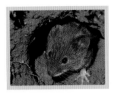 **burrow** hole or tunnel dug by an animal

 **litter** group of baby animals born from the same mother at the same time

 **mammal** warm-blooded animal that has a backbone, hair or fur, and gives birth to live babies that feed on milk from their mother

 **nocturnal** awake at night and asleep during the day

 **predator** animal that hunts other animals for food

Find out more

Books

Mice (Keeping Pets), Louise Spilsbury (Heinemann Library, 2007)

Rats and Mice (Pets Plus), Sally Morgan (Franklin Watts, 2011)

Websites

Learn how to care for pet mice at:
http://aspca.org/pet-care/small-pet-care/mouse-care

Discover more nocturnal animals at:
http://bbc.co.uk/nature/adaptations/Nocturnality

Index

babies 14
barns 17
bats 7
berries 10
buildings 17
burrows 9
cats 13
claws 4
diseases 21
droppings 18
ears 4

eyes 22
fields 8
food 10, 11, 12, 13, 20
forests 8
foxes 7, 12
fruit 11
garages 17
gardens 8
hedgehogs 7
homes 8, 17

humans 11, 13
insects 10
leaves 9
legs 4
litters 14
mammals 4
nests 9, 16, 17
noses 22
nuts 10
owls 7, 12
predators 12, 13

roots 10
rubbish 11, 20
seeds 10
sticks 9
tails 4, 22
vegetables 11
weasels 12
whiskers 22